Get Out of the Pews

Let the Lord Tell You What to Do!

By: Tatiana Whigham

Copyright © 2016. All rights reserved.

No part of this publication may be reproduced, stored in a retrieval system or transmitted in any way by any means, electronic, mechanical, photocopy, recording or otherwise, without the prior permission of the author except as provided by USA copyright law.

All characters appearing in this work are fictitious. Any resemblance to real persons, living or dead, is purely coincidental.

The opinions expressed by the author are not necessarily those of Revival Waves of Glory Books & Publishing.

Published by Revival Waves of Glory Books & Publishing

PO Box 596| Litchfield, Illinois 62056 USA

www.revivalwavesofgloryministries.com

Revival Waves of Glory Books & Publishing is committed to excellence in the publishing industry.

Book design Copyright © 2016 by Revival Waves of Glory Books & Publishing. All rights reserved.

Published in the United States of America

Paperback:

Table of Contents

Author's Notes 4

PART I: *GO* 7

Chapter 1: Recycling stops here! 8

Chapter 2: The Power of Your 'Go' 11

PART 2: *MAKE* 14

Chapter 3: Faith Without Works Is Dead 15

Chapter 4: The Martha Syndrome 21

PART 3: BAPTIZE 23

Chapter 5: The Process of Growth 24

Chapter 6: The System Still Works 30

PART 4: *TEACH* 38

Chapter 7: You can't teach what you don't know 39

The Parable of the Workers in the Vineyard 41

Author's Notes

Greetings to each and every one of you! I'm so glad that you've taken out both the time and the opportunity to read this piece. Of that, I'm grateful. I truly hope that you enjoy reading it as much as I've enjoyed writing it.

Now I've been traveling with the ministry for quite some time now, and it deeply saddens me that so many people follow the same religious routines day in and day out. Praise the Lord on Sunday mornings and sometimes on Wednesday nights, and the rest of the week many of us unconsciously begin to tune God out. We become just like the Pharisees in Luke 6 where we proclaim (more or less with our actions rather than our words) that Jesus is only Lord on Sunday mornings, and that He only has the power to deliver inside of the four walls that we call church. We only comfort people on Sundays. We only encourage and communicate with our neighbors on bible nights. But where is the healing, the words of wisdom, and the love of Jesus shown to one another every other day of the week?

People still need you to lift them up in prayer on Tuesdays. The sick and shut-in still need to see your faces on Thursdays. Our children still need spiritual guidance on Fridays. It's a known fact that people can go to church with the same people for years on end and still aren't able to recall one another's names, birthdays, likes and dislikes, or even where they stay. It's like we're living in a season where we're proclaiming Christ, but we're forgetting how to live like Him.

With that said, I hope that you enjoy the read. GOD BLESS!!!!!

Matthew 28: 19-20 (NKJV)

". . .Go therefore and make disciples of all the nations, baptizing them in the name of the Father and the of the Son and of the Holy Spirit, teaching them to observe all things that I have commanded you; and lo, I am with you always, even to the end of the age." Amen.

    Verb usage: Go, Make, Baptize, and Teach

PART I: *GO*

Chapter 1:
Recycling stops here!

A few days ago, I went to visit my great-grandma. Being of old age and highly stuck in her ways, there's one golden rule: 'You don't come to Mema's house empty handed. It's a B.Y.O. (Bring Your Own) affair.' So that day being pretty hungry myself, I brought some food. We had KFC chicken with a side of mashed potatoes and a side of green beans. As we sat down to eat, I began to distribute the utensils (the plates, the forks, and the napkins). That night, we ate, talked, and ate some more. When we finished, I knew that it would be my job to clear the table. Since everything was plastic, there would be no dish washing for me, so I started to throw everything away.

Watching in shock, my grandma asked me, 'Child, what are you doing.' Feeling confused, I replied anyway, 'I'm clearing the table.'

Getting up, my great-grandma then said, 'Child this ain't the city. We don't throw anything away here. Give the scraps to the cats and clean the forks?'

'Why mema?'

'Child, we can use them again.'

Feeling defeated, I retrieve the materials from the trash.

Some of you may find this pointless or even silly, but believe me, I did too. But time brings about a change. I didn't understand it then, but I understand it now. My great-grandma is 98 years old. She grew up at the tail end of

World War I, in the heart of the great depression, through World War II, and even Vietnam. Being on the farm most of her life, she was never a soldier, but she was always taught how to survive. And growing up in her era, you didn't just throw things away. You recycled them.

In much of the same way, we 'recycle' Christians in the house of God. We go to the same church with the same people week after week and year after year. We preach to the same people. We encourage the same people. We pray for the same people. Prophecy is no longer honored as a gift, because we are prophesying to the same people about the same situations. And yet and still, if truth be told, many of these people still remain unchanged. People are still carrying the same sins to the altar. People are still part-taking in the same lifestyles. People are still running and shouting with the Holy Ghost but walk outside of the church doors cussing and swearing. Something is definitely wrong!

We're taking old habits, old sins, and old problems to the cross again and again. It's gotten to the point that we're no longer ministering, we're recycling. In Mark 2:17, Jesus says, '. . .Those who are well have no need of a physician, but those who are sick. I did not come to call the righteous, but sinners to repentance.' In other words, we can't keep recycling the saved to the point that we lose sight of the lost and broken-hearted.

In the last commission (Matthew 28:19-20), the first thing that Jesus tells His disciples is to Go! But what actually happens is that we don't 'Go' anywhere. We become so busy with the pressures of our own life (our families, our jobs, our school work, and even our 'church' business) to the point that we as body have stopped visiting the sick, the widows, the prison-bound, and the orphans. And unconsciously on a daily basis, we make things more about 'us' rather than about 'God!'

God didn't save us to save ourselves day in and day out. He saves us and blesses us so that in return, we'll be a blessing to others. 'Too much given, much is required (Luke 12:48).'

Chapter 2:
The Power of Your 'Go'

One of the most difficult concepts that even I had to obtain while writing this study is that the 'going' is not just a command, it's a test.

Before God could bless Abraham, Abraham first had to 'go' out from his family and his home. Before God could bless Moses, Moses had to 'go' to Pharaoh. Before God blessed the children of Israel with the promised land, they first had to 'go' through the wilderness. Your 'going' may not always look good, it may not always feel good, but it will work out for your good. When you 'go,' you leave your comfort zone, not really knowing what's in front of you but trusting Jesus with every step. But most importantly when you 'go', you begin to activate your faith and its teachings.

> As a teacher, I used to do this thing. To encourage children to use their imaginations and think outside of the box, I would gather a whole bunch of odd materials and give them the timed-task of creating a structure (whether it be a boat, a building, an edible dish, or etc). These items would be things that would never go together ordinarily (like peanut butter, hot mustard, coconut pieces, lemons, rice crispy cereal, or etc.). When I say 'go' and start the timer, each student would have the task of not only creating, but also discovering. Some may discover that they like cooking. Some may discover that they like building things. Some may discover that they

have artistic skills. Some may discover that they work-well under pressure. It's in the process that the students begin to discover something on the inside of them that ordinarily would have never been noticed.

In this same way, God uses our 'going' seasons to allow us to see gifts, and talents in ourselves that we probably never would have found on our own.

Putting this into prospective, you will never meet the people that God has made you to reach still sitting on the mercy pews interceding for yourself. You will never meet the opportunities and the doors of ministries waiting for you if you don't first 'go' to meet them.

Know that my 'go' may not be your 'go.' It was my 'go' to write. Two years ago, you could've never told me that by now, I will have written and published more than five books. It was my 'go' to start a youth department at my church. Never would I have believed that God would use the youth department to impact the public enough to open events and functions for all of the children in the community. Your 'go' may be cooking your neighbor a bite to eat. Your 'go' may be visiting a church member at a nursing home. Your 'go' may be tutoring children on your off-times. The only person who knows your 'go' is you. But one thing I can tell you that in whatever your 'go' is, there is an opportunity waiting for you.

I've had the pleasure of meeting a man. He'd spent over 15 or more years strung out on drugs and alcohol. In the process, he walked away from a good job, a wife, and even his children. For years, he slumped through life living a hot mess and sleeping on city streets. When God delivered him, he had experienced abandonment, hopelessness, and finally, redemption. He would often tell me, 'Tot, a smile goes a long way.' So following God's voice, he would walk up to every person that he saw, smile and say, 'Hi.' He started off doing this to random people at local stores. Then later on, he would block out a whole Saturday just to walk door to door doing the same thing, smiling and saying 'Hi.' This seems so meniscal and pointless, but that was his 'go' (to encourage as many people as he could with one word and a smile). God used his 'go,' and gave him an outreach ministry. Now he has a crew of 40/50 people smiling, greeting, feeding, and even ministering the word of God to people living in the streets. Weeks at a time, he goes from city to city and neighborhood to neighborhood meeting people face-to-face with Jesus.

You don't know the power of your 'go.' So please, don't count it out!

PART 2: *MAKE*

Chapter 3:
Faith Without Works Is Dead

One of my favorite parables in the bible deals with the workers in the Vineyard (Matthew 20). This guy was in desperate need of people willing to work his vineyard, so early in the morning he goes out searching for workers. Initially, only a few come out. Seeing that there is more work to be done, the man goes back out looking for more help and manages to pull in a few more. And this continues until the close of the day which in my language means it's time to get paid! Surprisingly, the man pays everyone the same wage.

Remembering how I felt the very first time I read this passage, I wanted to side with the vineyard workers, because I've experienced in the workforce having the frustration of working twice as hard and twice as long as another individual and still receiving the same pay. I've experienced the dilemma of not wanting to give all of my energy, all of my efforts, and all of my being because I felt like I was under appreciated. I can relate to the vineyard workers, because in 2 Thessalonians (3:10) it says, 'if a man doesn't work, he don't eat.' So, I understand where the vineyard workers are coming from. But what Jesus is trying to point out in this passage is that the significance is not when or even how long each man worked, it's the fact that the work was done. You see, I may have been one of the workers to come in early, but by myself, I can't reach from one row to another, that job belongs to someone else. Even though I may have come a little earlier, you may pick faster than I do. Even though I may have come a little earlier, I still need you to complete the job. You can't do what I can do, and I can't do what's left for you to do.

Putting this into prospective, I can only teach who God has made me to reach. There are people specifically assigned to you, your job, your school, your family, and even in your community that are waiting for you to put your faith to work. There are people waiting for you to speak a word of life. There are people waiting for you to show them that service is not beneath the called. There are people waiting for you to show them that righteous living is still possible. There are people, there are people. . . .and the most amazing thing about this is that you have the ability to touch someone's life and never even know it, but by faith, it's done.

"Go your way; behold, I send you out as lambs among wolves. . .But whatever city you enter, and they do not receive you, go out into its streets and say, 'The very dust of your city which clings to us we wipe off against you. Nevertheless, know this, that the kingdom of God has come near you.'" (Luke 10: 3; 10-11)

It is our job as disciples to take the gospel to the streets, but many people fail at this for one of two reasons: Failure of Duty or Fear.

1) **Failure of Duty:** Many people in the Christian faith feel that it's not their job to spread the gospel abroad; in their minds, it's the job of those in leadership. This concept is crippling to the faith of the believer. Spreading the gospel is simply you

spreading the power of your testimony. If you don't tell what you've been through, then how are people going to know that they can make it through. Hallelujah Lord! How different would Jesus' ministry have been if the leapers didn't tell that they've been healed? How different would Jesus' ministry have been if the blind man never told anyone that he had received sight? How different would our faith be had the Hebrews boys' never talked about walking through the fire? How different would our faith be had the children of Israel not talked about the Red Sea? It's the power of your testimony that gives life to the gospel. We live in a world today where many people feel that the stories of the bible are in fact fables. The only truth to the power of God in their minds is what they've seen Him do.

    a) Over the years, I've had a few people ask me why I believe the stories in the bible. My answer to them is this, 'I believe that Jesus healed the blind man (Luke 18: 35-43), because He healed my sight as a child. I believe that Jesus can heal the sick (Luke 17: 11-19), because I was there when the doctor's told my family that my brother (who's terminally ill due to an incurable lung disease, CF) would never live to see the age of 21. He's alive and well today by the grace of God and about to turn 30. I believe that the Lord parted the Red Sea (Exodus 14), because I've had times in my life where God made a way out of no way for me. I believe that Jesus walked with the Hebrew Boys' through Fire Furnace (Daniel 3: 19-25), because I've been in an accident where everybody said that there's no way that I could've made it out alive. But today, I'm alive and well, with not a scratch to show for it. I believe that Jesus healed the demon possessed man (Luke 8: 26-39), because I've watched as He healed my loved one from years of alcohol and drug abuse. I believe that the Lord brought Lazarus back from the grave (John 11: 38-44), because when I was born, I came out of the womb dead on arrival. But the Lord saw fit to keep me. I believe, because I've seen.' Others will believe, because of what you've seen. If the Lord has done anything for you, you ought to run and tell it. Tell somebody that you've beat addiction. Tell somebody that you've survived cancer. Tell somebody that the Lord healed your marriage. Tell somebody that the Lord watched over your child. Tell somebody that you've beat depression. Tell somebody about Jesus!

b) I heard a man say once, that he used to practice homosexuality, and that he struggled with it for many years. He wanted to change his lifestyle, but he had never heard of anybody being delivered from it (and so in his mind, the enemy had convinced him that deliverance from such a lifestyle was impossible). What he didn't know, was that there were several people sitting in the pews right there in the congregation who had been through the same thing. But they never said a word, because they were ashamed of it. My point is this, you can't be ashamed of where you've been. It's your experience that's going to comfort somebody, going to deliver somebody, going to heal somebody. You don't know the power of your testimony. Your testimony can encourage someone who's on the verge of giving up to hang in there just a little while longer.

c) Paul explains this point best in 2 Corinthians (1: 3-4), when he states that, '. . .who comforts us in our tribulation that we may be able to comfort those who are in any trouble. . ." We're blessed with the deliverance to deliver others. God comforts us, so that in turn, we can stand in the gap and comfort someone else. God is not just working on us for His health. He's shaping us, molding us, and training us to be a support system for others.

2) **Fear:** Many believers fail to spread the gospel out of the fear of being rejected. And the reason why they fear this is because they unconsciously place value on the acceptance of others. So in other words, it's the mind frame that if you don't accept my belief, my word loses it's value. When in reality, this frame of thinking is completely false. In Luke 10:10-11, Jesus informs his disciples that people will reject you. People will refuse to listen to you. People will slam a

door in your face. People will. . .But Jesus (in so many words) tells His followers, don't sweat the small stuff. If people refuse to listen, that's ok, just go to the next person. The point of the gospel is not whether or not people will *receive* you. The point is that each person gets a chance to *hear* you whether they like it or not.

    a. "For God has not given us a spirit of fear, but of power and of love and of a sound mind." (2 Timothy 1: 7) This verse, in particular, is so moving to me, because in spite of all that I go through, it reminds me that Jesus gave me power. Through Christ, I have the power to overcome any obstacle, the power to love even when it hurts, the power to smile when I really feel like crying, the power to stand on God's word in the midst. . . . the power, the power. It's by this power that Jesus has called us to speak the gospel boldly, 'being not ashamed of the testimony of our Lord. . . (2 Timothy 1:8)."

Chapter 4:
The Martha Syndrome

'Now it happened as they went that He entered a certain village; and a certain woman named Martha welcomed Him into her house. And she had a sister called Mary, who also sat at Jesus' feet and heard His word. But Martha was distracted with much serving, and she approached Him and said, "Lord, do You not care that my sister has left me to serve alone? Therefore tell her to help me." And Jesus answered and said to her, "Martha, Martha, you are worried and troubled about many things. But one thing is needed and Mary has chosen that good part, which will not be taken away from her. (Luke 10: 38-41 NKJV)'

In this passage, Martha welcomes Jesus. But when Jesus comes in, Martha becomes distracted with things that seem to be important and really aren't. She's distracted with cooking. She's distracted with preparing for company. She's distracted. Martha represents us all. Similar to Martha, we invite Jesus into our lives, but when He comes in, we give Him poor excuses of service. 'Jesus I can't hug that homeless man, because I have on my church clothes.' 'Jesus, I can't stop and help that young lady fix her flat tire, because I'll be late for church.' 'Jesus, I can't go sit with that woman who just lost her child, because it's my only day off.' You see, we become so heavenly bound that we are no longer any Earthly good, this is what I like to call the Martha Syndrome.

Why is this? Well, if truth be told, many believers really don't know how to distinguish service from divine worship. They view both components as a unit rather than separate, but equally important parts of our belief system. When I was growing up as a young girl in the church, I can remember many people on various occasions say, post, or tweet on Sunday Mornings that they 'were going to serve the Lord.' One Sunday morning, my pastor touched on the topic, and he said, 'we *worship* inside of the church, and we serve *outside* of the church.' Sunday mornings are not take-alls, 'I've taken all that I need from God, let me be on my way.' Sunday mornings are fueling sessions, 'Sunday mornings give you the strength and the discipline to endure the trials of life so that you can be in the world, but not of the world (John 17:16). Service is an outside experience. But if there is no true worship, then there can be no real service. In other words, you can't show the love of Jesus Christ if you're not connected with Him.

Part 3: Baptize

Chapter 5:
The Process of Growth

You know, I like to watch plants grow. It's just so amazing to me how so much can come from such tiny seeds. Apple trees, peaches trees, pear trees, all start from little seeds. Grape vines, watermelons, potatoes, tomatoes, and wheat, all start from tiny seeds. So much production comes from such little investment.

I remember the first plant that I ever owned. I was in my junior year in college. In my particular dorm, pets were not allowed, but we could have as many plants as we'd like. It was during a dorm activity that the dorm manager gave all of the residents' seeds and pots. We painted the pots ourselves, put in the soil, mixed in the seeds, and that was it. Each plant came with minor instructions of the periods of watering. Some plants needed to be watered every day, while others needed to be watered every other day. But the dorm Manager made it clear that without constant watering (whether it be too much or too little), the plant itself would die. So, I took my plant with enthusiasm. Not really having any ventilation in the dorm, I put the plant in the bathroom where it could get optimal sunlight. I named the plant Bessie-Mae. The first day that I watered it, nothing. The second day that I watered it, still nothing. This process went on and on for about a week or two. Then one day it happened, a little green shrub uprooted itself from the soil. And from that point on, Bessie-Mae grew and grew. I was so excited that each day I would measure Bessie-Mae to make sure that I didn't miss a moment of the process. But then one day, I went on a trip for a whole week with a campus group. When I returned, I rushed into my room, dropped my bags, and ran to visit Bessie-Mae. But when I got there, Bessie-Mae was gone. Her pot was still there. The soil was still there, but the plant itself had curled up and died. This devastated me so much to the fact that I spent the entire following week trying to revive it without any success.

I've said all that to say this. Every person that we come in contact with are seeds with potential harvest sitting on the instead of them. My harvest may not be your harvest, but we all have a harvest sitting patiently on the inside of us. Every time that we go to a person and say, 'God is good,' we're planting a seed. Every time that we go to a person and say, 'Jesus loves you,' we're planting a seed. Every little nugget of the Christian faith that we deposit into somebody else's life is a seed that has been planted.

Now realize that just like in my story, Bessie-Mae didn't sprout out the first day. Likewise, people coming into the faith will not sprout out immediately either. But each day that the seed is watered, the growth of the seed is in process. The part that I like here is that we have to realize that like seeds, people coming to believe are tiny in faith and can at any point be deterred from the process. That's why we as believers have to plant seeds in **_good_** ground. Know that mentioning the name of Jesus does not make your soil ***good*** ground. It's the evidence of Jesus that makes the soil ***good*** ground. I don't believe that God is good because you told me. 'I believe that He's good, because when I hungry, you fed me. When I was thirsty, you gave me something to drink. When I was homeless, you took me in. When I was sick, you came by my bedside. When I was in prison, you didn't forget about me (a reference to Matthew 25:41-46).' I believe that Jesus is good, because He loved me enough to show up through you in my life. Every time that you see someone, you have a God-given opportunity to encourage, to uplift, and to speak deliverance into someone else's life.

"I planted, Apollos watered, but God gave the increase (1 Corinthians 3:6)."

Know that everything that you do can, in fact, benefit the kingdom of God. Your words are important. The prayers that you pray are important. The hymns that you uplift are important. The songs that you sing are important. Everything that we say and do have the potential to encourage someone to give his/her life to Christ on a daily basis. So why might I ask are people not flocking to the church? Why are people not running to the pews? I'll tell you why. It's because believers in today's time don't really grasp the importance of advertising Jesus on a daily basis. We can have an hour conversation and not even mention the name, Jesus. We can work 8 hours plus on a job, and not even tell someone that Jesus still saves. We are asleep to the fact that Christ still shows up outside of church walls. We are asleep to the fact that every day, we are laborers in God's kingdom. We get so caught up in our own lives that we forget to encourage someone to lift up the name of Jesus in theirs.

I read this story once that a minister was working late at the church and decided to call his wife and tell her that he would be late for dinner. When he called the house a man answered the phone. He said 'Hello?' The man replied, 'Hello.' Not really knowing what else to say, the minister gathered his words and asked, 'Is my wife there by any chance?' The man answered and said 'No, no she's not.' Unsure of how to take this, the minister said, 'Oh, okay well I'll call back later.' For the next thirty minutes, the minister was puzzled by the fact that a man at that very moment was at his house. He had never known his wife to be unfaithful, that never even crossed his mind. He knew that he'd been busy for the last few months working terribly long hours, but he loved his wife and he wanted to make sure that she still knew that. Unable to concentrate, the minister left his work and headed to his house. When he got there, he walked in expecting to see the man that he'd spoken with on the phone. But all he saw was his wife preparing the dinner table. When she saw him, the wife said, 'Wow, you're here mighty early. I thought that I was going to have to eat dinner by myself again tonight.' Really puzzled at this point the minister questions his wife about the conversation that he'd had with a man just a few minutes earlier. The wife completely denies the fact that anyone besides her had been in the house and she stressed the fact that she had not received a call from him that night. Willing to prove his point, the minister drove back to the office with his wife to show her on the call log that he had called. When the wife looked at the call log, she burst out laughing and replied, 'Honey, you didn't call me. Look! Our number is 555-0618 not 555-0638.' In complete disbelief, the minister looked at his phone and true enough, he had called the wrong number. Feeling rather embarrassed, the minister called the number back to apologize to the young gentlemen that was on the other end. When the man picked up the line and listened as the minister gave his deepest heartfelt apology he calmly replied, 'Don't feel bad minister, you were the answer to a prayer. When you called, I was about to take my own life and end everything. In one last plea, I prayed to God that if He was really who He said that He was, could He give me a sign. At that exact moment, you called me, and as I looked at the caller ID, I saw the words '*God Still Saves.*' When the minister heard that, he immediately began to pray and witness to the young man on the other end.

You see, we never know how we can help others. The minister intended to call his wife, but God allowed him to dial the wrong number, so that God would be able to reach someone who needed Him at the time. You see, the name of the church was *God Still Saves Church of Christ*, that's why the caller ID read *God Still Saves.* God used this minor detail to deliver a young man in his time of need.

With that one mistake, God used the minister to plant a seed of hope with this young man and water it when he witnessed to him. This is the power of our God. That's why we plant and we water, but it is God who gives the increase.

The growth of a believer is indeed a process, that's why God has given us the opportunity to plant multiple seeds daily with each person that we come in contact with. Just like a field of crops, we may not reap the harvest today, but when we do, we will reap them in His timing.

Chapter 6:
The System Still Works

". . .the word of God came to John the son of Zacharias in the wilderness. And he went into all the region around the Jordan, preaching a baptism of repentance from the remission of sins, (Luke 3:2-3 NKJV)"

One of the earliest examples of a believer who accepted the call from Christ and began to operate in his 'Go' is John the Baptist. I love his story, because John the Baptist walked away from a life of royalty (Luke 1: 5-25) and comfort to ultimately become homeless with wild hair, trashy clothes, and bugs with honey for food (Mark 1:6). His father was a priest and had the best of the best. Instead of preaching from a pulpit, John the Baptist chose to preach from the streets. You're talking about sacrifice! John the Baptist traded steak dinners for Garbage soufflé. But the bible tells me that he went. When he went, all of Judea and Jerusalem came to hear him. This fact moves me because it highlights the fact that if I don't 'go,' how are people ever going to know. Had John the Baptist not gone into the streets preaching on the level of common people with common problems, how would those people have heard about Jesus? The reason why we are not seeing such an outpour of people coming to the house of God is because the people of God are not GOING OUT! In order for people to come in, the believers have to GO OUT! When we go out, people see that somebody has stood in their shoes before. When John the Baptist went out, he proved to people that he knew what it was like to live on the streets.

He knew what it was like to be without. He knew what it was like to not know where your next meal was going to come from. He knew what it was like to be looked down on. He knew, he knew, he knew. . . .But in today's time, we have so many people highlighting their glories and not really telling people their stories. When people see where you've been, they have faith that they CAN! Keep in mind; to some people you are the only visible evidence of what God can do.

"Then Peter said to them, 'Repent, and let every one of you be baptized in the name of Jesus Christ for the remission of sins; and you shall receive the gift of the Holy Spirit. For the promise is to you and to your children, and to all who are afar off, as many as the Lord our God will call.' And with many other words he testified and exhorted them, saying, 'Be saved from this perverse generation.' Then those who gladly received his word were baptized; and that day about three thousand souls were added to them (Acts 2:38-41 NKJV)."

I love this portion of Acts, because for the first in the New Testament, Peter was REAL. Being one of the twelve disciples, Peter had the opportunity to preach to people daily. But on this day, Peter's testimony was so impactful because, for the first time in his ministry, Peter was preaching something that he knew. He could tell people that Christ would forgive their sins, because even when he denied Christ 3 times, Christ still forgave him. He could tell people about the power of the Holy Ghost, because the Holy Ghost was finally in him. When he preached this sermon, he didn't dress it up, tailor it, nor did he sugar-coat it. He preached the gospel not to be seen, but to be heard by the soul that needed it most. And that day, 3,000 people came to Christ. 3,000 people made the decision to make Jesus the Lord and Savior of their life because he preached what he knew. He could tell them where he's been. He could tell them that Jesus would pick them up. He could tell them that Jesus would be a bridge over troubled water. He could tell it, because he believed it.

But in today's time, we can't call people to repent of their sins, because we're still living in ours. We can't call people to lay down every weight that so easily besets them (Hebrew 12:1), because we are still walking around chained. If you want people to come to Christ, you first have to make the decision that Jesus is Lord. If bills are due, He's still Lord. If you're sick and can't get well, He's still Lord. If your children have gone astray, He's still Lord. If you're sitting down at the fork of life and don't know which way to go, He's still Lord. In order to baptize others, you have to accept the baptism in yourself. Colossians tells us that through baptism we are buried with Him (putting off the old man) and through faith, we are risen with Him (Colossians 2:11-12). But the reason why we can't effectually teach baptism, is because some of us have not thrown off the ways of the old man. Some of us are still lying, that's the old man. Some of us are still gossiping, that's the old man. Some of us are murdering others daily with the words that we speak, that's the old man. Some of us can't be content with what God gives us because we're walking around jealous of our neighbors, that's the old man. God's calling for a church without a spot or a wrinkle, and in order to be spotless, we have to be new!

So how do we get back to this place of true anointing? By using the 'System.' In Luke 10, Jesus sends out the disciples for the very first time as told by scripture. Before doing so, He gives them key instructions on how to maintain amongst the people. He says:

> (Then He said to them, "The harvest truly is great, but the laborers are few; therefore pray the Lord of the harvest to send out laborers into His harvest. Go your way; behold, I send you out as lambs among wolves. Carry neither money bag, knapsack, nor sandals; and greet no one along the road. But whatever house you enter, first say, 'Peace to this house.' And if a son of peace is there, your peace will rest on it; if not, it will return to you. And remain in the same house, eating and drinking such things as they give, for the laborer is worthy of his wages. Do not go from house to house. Whatever city you enter, and they receive you, eat such things as are set before you. And heal the sick there, and say to them, 'The kingdom of God has come near to you.' But whatever city you enter, and they do not receive you, go out into its streets and say, 'The very dust of your city which clings to us we wipe off against you. Nevertheless know this, that the kingdom of God has come near you.'" [Luke 10: 2-11])

In this passage of scripture, Jesus specifically outlines how He wants His disciples to go about spreading the gospel. This is Jesus' specific instructions on how to take the gospel to the streets. He starts off by saying that we should pray to the Lord to send out laborers. This part is particularly special to me, because it magnifies the fact that no one person can draw everybody. We are specifically designed to teach the people that God made us to reach. I can't, no matter how hard I try, get through spiritually to my brother. That's okay, just pray that the Lord send's the right laborer to him. I can't, no matter how hard I try, get through to my mother. That's okay, just pray that the Lord send's the right laborer to her. I can't reach, I can't reach. . . .That's okay, just pray that the Lord sends the right laborer. So the first key factor is to recognize whether or not you are the *RIGHT* laborer.

The next key point that Jesus points out is that we should go our way, carry nothing, and greet no one along the way. To put this into plain terms, we are to lean and to depend on God to supply our needs all the while staying clear of distractions. The bible says 'greet no one.' Why would Jesus say this if Greeting people is such a normal thing? Because Jesus knows that when we do things that we feel are justified (though these things may seem good) we actually get into things that distract us from our purpose. For instance, if I'm told to go to the grocery and buy orange juice. I may get to the store and see laundry detergent on sale (and think, oh we need that), I may see some tissue on sale (buy one, get one free), and so on. You see, it's possible that I can still walk into a store, leave with a cart full and still forget that I was supposed to be getting orange Juice. We as believers are this way spiritually. We have so many things in life competing for our attention other than the Lord. We have finance obligations, family issues, personal hurts and pains, job stressors, and so much more begging us to pay attention to them and lay our responsibility to the Kingdom down. That's why Jesus told the disciples to go their way and don't stop. Jesus was trying to stress the importance of STAYING FOCUSED on this journey.

The next step in the system is called, 'Try the Spirit by the Spirit.' Jesus specifically instructed each disciple to test the spirit of the houses in which they entered into with just a simple phrase 'Peace to this house.' Judging by the response that follows such comment, the disciples would know who would receive them and who wasn't. This is the part that causes many Christians to stumble. Many Christians spend too much time trying to save people who don't want to be saved. Change will only come when the believer is ready to receive it. The bible tells us in Galatians 6:1, "Brethren, if a man is overtaken in any trespass, you who are spiritual restore such a one in a spirit of gentleness, considering yourself lest you also be tempted." Remember, we are flesh as well. At this point Jesus is cautioning them not to try to restore a spirit before it's time lest they themselves be put to the test. In plain terms, if you run into someone who has no intentions of hearing the word of God, that's ok just move on. If you run into someone who is stubborn in his/her spiritual belief, that's fine just move on. We as believers cannot pressure someone into serving the Lord, this is a choice that they must make within themselves. We SHARE Jesus; we don't SELL Jesus!

Finally in the last portion, Jesus deals with REJECTION. Many believers feel that just because he/she is speaking the truth, that people will not reject them. If people refused to listen to Jesus, what makes us any different? But what happens a lot of times is that we as believers place value on the people who reject us. We can have a hundred people praise us, but if one person critiques us negatively, that one comment may weigh on us all night.

Jesus is telling His followers, 'Don't sweat the small stuff. Just brush it off and keep moving.' The bible tells us that life is but a vapor. Because of such, we can't afford to waste time and energy on a negative response. In order to effectively work the system, we have to first work our faith and LET SOME THINGS GO!!!!!

This is Jesus' system: pray for direction (am I the right person for the job), depend on God to supply all of your needs, stay on track and don't get distracted, test the spirit by the spirit, accept rejection because it will come, and let go of the things that don't matter. This is a proven system. We know it works. So in our own lives, we have to remember to use the system (Jesus' system), because yes, it still works. But in today's time, we have too many people trying to re-invent the wheel (in attempts of finding new ways to draw people to church). You can't draw a spirit somewhere that he/she doesn't want to be. We have far too many churches advertising Christ, but not living Christ. Churches that post on facebook, post on twitter, put ads in the Newspaper but still can't find the time to visit the sick and shut-in. Churches that will deck the halls of the sanctuary, but won't spend one red cent on feeding the homeless. The work of the kingdom is outside the house of God, not in it. We worship the Lord in the house, and we serve Him in the streets. We have far too many churches trying to bring the world to the church (new music, new attire, new hymns, new traditions, new religious views, new, new, new. . . .). We as Christians are supposed to be lights of the world (Matthew 5:14) living in the world but not of the world (Romans 12:2). We are made to stand out. We are made to be separate. If we do what the world does, what's the need of the world coming to Christ? There is still power in your testimony. There is still power in your praise. There is still power in taking the gospel to the streets. There's still power! Stick to the system, because IT STILL WORKS!!!

Baptism is the choice of a person who's finally made the decision to give up his/her life to Christ, but how can we draw people like this if we're not fully in Christ ourselves. We as believers have to stop treading life lukewarm (Revelation 3:16) and really make the distinct choice to live for Christ fully. Enough playing around, it's time for us as believers to throw off the old man and walk into our season of 'new (new talk, new walk, new mindset, new goals, new dreams, new, new, new. . .   .).' It's time out for the 'Imitating-Christian' or the 'Just-Enough-believer.' It's time to be REAL!

Each time that we preach the word, speak our testimony, or even encourage someone on a sunny day, we are lifting up the name of Jesus. And Jesus tells us, that if He is lifted up, He'll draw all men unto Him (John 12:32). Our job is to lift Him up through our talk, our actions, and even our living. At this point in your life, are you really lifting Jesus up? Are you glorifying Him in the things that you say and do?

Part 4: *Teach*

Chapter 7:
You can't teach what you don't know

"Study to shew thyself approved unto God, a workman that needeth not to be ashamed, rightly dividing the word of truth. (2 Timothy 2:15 KJV)."

In today's time, we have too many people trying to graduate from the Christian Faith. You can get degrees in Theology, read the bible over twice, preach for 20 years and still get new understanding from the word of God. Why? Because the scriptures of God are both living and active (Hebrews 4:12), always standing ready to correct, to rebuke, and to guide us into righteous living (2Timothy 3:16). Because we only know in part (1 Corinthians 13:9), we are constantly dependent on God for both new revelation and new understanding.

This is why Jesus charges us to study the word. Many people are so used to equivocating Satan to a non-believer that they forget that Lucifer (Satan) was once an Angel of God himself (Ezekiel 28: 12-19; Isaiah 14:12-15; Revelations 12:7-9). According to the bible, Satan was not just an average Angel; he was perfect. I don't know if you get this, but you and I can never be perfect no matter how hard we try. The bible tells us that our best is to God but filthy rags (Isaiah 64:6). So when it comes to the word of God in verbiage Satan has us beat hands down. The only thing that we have to resist the deception of the enemy is Jesus. See Satan can talk like God, but he can't love like Him. It is our job to study the word and hide it in our hearts (Psalms 119:11), so when we need it most, it will breathe life into us.

The bible tells us that the word of God is foolishness to those who are perishing, but it is power to those who believe (1 Corinthians 1:18). Satan fights us in our minds through deception of the word, but Jesus Christ fights for us in our souls when we believe. Your faith is the very weapon that you use to shield yourself from the attacks of the enemy (Ephesians 6:16), and the word of God is what you use to fight the enemy off (Ephesians 6:17). But if you haven't read anything, than you don't know anything. If you don't know that God is good (Psalms 136:1), then you won't know how to be content in the midst of your situation (without the knowledge of the word, the enemy will deceive you into to believing that God has left you). If you don't know that God is able (Ephesians 3:20), then you can by no way believe that He will rescue you in your time of need (without the knowledge of the word, the enemy will deceive you into believing that God has forgotten about you).

You can't believe what your spirit has not yet received. That's why we are called to study. You can never graduate from the kingdom of God, that's why you have to study.

Spiritual Text Glossary:

1) Matthew 20: 1-16

The Parable of the Workers in the Vineyard

20 For the kingdom of heaven is like unto a man that is an householder, which went out early in the morning to hire labourers into his vineyard. ² And when he had agreed with the labourers for a penny a day, he sent them into his vineyard. ³ And he went out about the third hour, and saw others standing idle in the marketplace, ⁴ And said unto them; Go ye also into the vineyard, and whatsoever is right I will give you. And they went their way. ⁵ Again he went out about the sixth and ninth hour, and did likewise. ⁶ And about the eleventh hour he went out, and found others standing idle, and saith unto them, Why stand ye here all the day idle? ⁷ They say unto him, because no man hath hired us. He saith unto them, Go ye also into the vineyard; and whatsoever is right, that shall ye receive. ⁸ So when even was come, the lord of the vineyard saith unto his steward, Call the labourers, and give them their hire, beginning from the last unto the first. ⁹ And when they came that were hired about the eleventh hour, they received every man a penny. ¹⁰ But when the first came, they supposed that they should have received more; and they likewise received every man a penny. ¹¹ And when they had received it, they murmured against the good man of the house, ¹² Saying, These last have wrought but one hour, and thou hast made them equal unto us, which have

borne the burden and heat of the day. ¹³ But he answered one of them, and said, Friend, I do thee no wrong: didst not thou agree with me for a penny? ¹⁴ Take that thine is, and go thy way: I will give unto this last, even as unto thee. ¹⁵ Is it not lawful for me to do what I will with mine own? Is thine eye evil, because I am good? ¹⁶ So the last shall be first, and the first last: for many be called, but few chosen.

(KJV)

2) Luke 18: 35-43

A Blind Man Receives His Sight

³⁵ Then it happened, as He was coming near Jericho, that a certain blind man sat by the road begging. ³⁶ And hearing a multitude passing by, he asked what it meant. ³⁷ So they told him that Jesus of Nazareth was passing by. ³⁸ And he cried out, saying, "Jesus, Son of David, have mercy on me!"

³⁹ Then those who went before warned him that he should be quiet; but he cried out all the more, "Son of David, have mercy on me!"

⁴⁰ So Jesus stood still and commanded him to be brought to Him. And when he had come near, He asked him, ⁴¹ saying, "What do you want Me to do for you?"

He said, "Lord, that I may receive my sight."

⁴² Then Jesus said to him, "Receive your sight; your faith has made you well." ⁴³ And immediately he

received his sight, and followed Him, glorifying God. And all the people, when they saw *it,* gave praise to God.

(NKJV)

3) Luke 17: 11-19

   Ten Lepers Cleansed

   ¹¹ Now it happened as He went to Jerusalem that He passed through the midst of Samaria and Galilee. ¹² Then as He entered a certain village, there met Him ten men who were lepers, who stood afar off. ¹³ And they lifted up *their* voices and said, "Jesus, Master, have mercy on us!"

   ¹⁴ So when He saw *them,* He said to them, "Go, show yourselves to the priests." And so it was that as they went, they were cleansed.

   ¹⁵ And one of them, when he saw that he was healed, returned, and with a loud voice glorified God, ¹⁶ and fell down on *his* face at His feet, giving Him thanks. And he was a Samaritan.

   ¹⁷ So Jesus answered and said, "Were there not ten cleansed? But where *are* the nine? ¹⁸ Were there not any found who returned to give glory to God except this foreigner?" ¹⁹ And He said to him, "Arise, go your way. Your faith has made you well."

   (NKJV)

4) Exodus 14

   The Red Sea Crossing

14 Now the Lord spoke to Moses, saying: ²"Speak to the children of Israel, that they turn and camp before Pi Hahiroth, between Migdol and the sea, opposite Baal Zephon; you shall camp before it by the sea. ³For Pharaoh will say of the children of Israel, 'They *are* bewildered by the land; the wilderness has closed them in.' ⁴Then I will harden Pharaoh's heart, so that he will pursue them; and I will gain honor over Pharaoh and over all his army, that the Egyptians may know that I *am* the Lord." And they did so.

⁵Now it was told the king of Egypt that the people had fled, and the heart of Pharaoh and his servants was turned against the people; and they said, "Why have we done this, that we have let Israel go from serving us?" ⁶So he made ready his chariot and took his people with him. ⁷Also, he took six hundred choice chariots, and all the chariots of Egypt with captains over every one of them. ⁸And the Lord hardened the heart of Pharaoh king of Egypt, and he pursued the children of Israel; and the children of Israel went out with boldness. ⁹So the Egyptians pursued them, all the horses *and* chariots of Pharaoh, his horsemen and his army, and overtook them camping by the sea beside Pi Hahiroth, before Baal Zephon.

¹⁰And when Pharaoh drew near, the children of Israel lifted their eyes, and behold, the Egyptians marched after them. So they were very afraid, and the children of Israel cried out to the Lord. ¹¹Then they said to Moses, "Because *there were* no graves in Egypt, have you taken us away to die in the wilderness? Why have you so dealt with us, to bring

us up out of Egypt? ¹²*Is* this not the word that we told you in Egypt, saying, 'Let us alone that we may serve the Egyptians'? For *it would have been* better for us to serve the Egyptians than that we should die in the wilderness."

¹³ And Moses said to the people, "Do not be afraid. Stand still, and see the salvation of the Lord, which He will accomplish for you today. For the Egyptians whom you see today, you shall see again no more forever. ¹⁴ The Lord will fight for you, and you shall hold your peace."

¹⁵ And the Lord said to Moses, "Why do you cry to Me? Tell the children of Israel to go forward. ¹⁶ But lift up your rod, and stretch out your hand over the sea and divide it. And the children of Israel shall go on dry *ground* through the midst of the sea. ¹⁷ And I indeed will harden the hearts of the Egyptians, and they shall follow them. So I will gain honor over Pharaoh and over all his army, his chariots, and his horsemen. ¹⁸ Then the Egyptians shall know that I *am* the Lord, when I have gained honor for Myself over Pharaoh, his chariots, and his horsemen."

¹⁹ And the Angel of God, who went before the camp of Israel, moved and went behind them; and the pillar of cloud went from before them and stood behind them. ²⁰ So it came between the camp of the Egyptians and the camp of Israel. Thus it was a cloud and darkness *to the one,* and it gave light by night *to the other,* so that the one did not come near the other all that night.

²¹ Then Moses stretched out his hand over the sea; and the Lord caused the sea to go *back* by a strong east wind all that night, and made the sea into dry *land,* and the waters were divided. ²² So the children of Israel went into the midst of the sea on the dry *ground,* and the waters *were* a wall to them on their right hand and on their left. ²³ And the Egyptians pursued and went after them into the midst of the sea, all Pharaoh's horses, his chariots, and his horsemen.

²⁴ Now it came to pass, in the morning watch, that the Lord looked down upon the army of the Egyptians through the pillar of fire and cloud, and He troubled the army of the Egyptians. ²⁵ And He took off[a] their chariot wheels, so that they drove them with difficulty; and the Egyptians said, "Let us flee from the face of Israel, for the Lord fights for them against the Egyptians."

²⁶ Then the Lord said to Moses, "Stretch out your hand over the sea, that the waters may come back upon the Egyptians, on their chariots, and on their horsemen." ²⁷ And Moses stretched out his hand over the sea; and when the morning appeared, the sea returned to its full depth, while the Egyptians were fleeing into it. So the Lord overthrew the Egyptians in the midst of the sea. ²⁸ Then the waters returned and covered the chariots, the horsemen, *and* all the army of Pharaoh that came into the sea after them. Not so much as one of them remained. ²⁹ But the children of Israel had walked on dry *land* in the midst of the sea, and the waters *were* a wall to them on their right hand and on their left.

³⁰ So the Lord saved Israel that day out of the hand of the Egyptians, and Israel saw the Egyptians dead on the seashore. ³¹ Thus Israel saw the great work which the Lord had done in Egypt; so the people feared the Lord, and believed the Lord and His servant Moses.

(NKJV)

5) Daniel 3:19-25

Saved in Fiery Trial

¹⁹Then Nebuchadnezzar was full of fury, and the expression on his face changed toward Shadrach, Meshach, and Abed-Nego. He spoke and commanded that they heat the furnace seven times more than it was usually heated. ²⁰And he commanded certain mighty men of valor who *were* in his army to bind Shadrach, Meshach, and Abed-Nego, *and* cast *them* into the burning fiery furnace. ²¹Then these men were bound in their coats, their trousers, their turbans, and their *other* garments, and were cast into the midst of the burning fiery furnace. ²²Therefore, because the king's command was urgent, and the furnaces exceedingly hot, the flame of the fire killed those men who took up Shadrach, Meshach, and Abed-Nego. ²³And these three men, Shadrach, Meshach, and Abed-Nego, fell down bound into the midst of the burning fiery furnace.

²⁴Then King Nebuchadnezzar was astonished; and he rose in haste *and* spoke, saying to his counselors, "Did we not cast three men bound into the midst of the fire?"

They answered and said to the king, "True, O king."

²⁵"Look!" he answered, "I see four men loose, walking in the midst of the fire; and they are not hurt, and the form of the fourth is like the Son of God."[a]

(NKJV)

6) Luke 8: 26-39

A Demon-Possessed Man Healed

²⁶Then they sailed to the country of the Gadarenes,[a] which is opposite Galilee. ²⁷And when He stepped out on the land, there met Him a certain man from the city who had demons for a long time. And he wore no clothes,[b] nor did he live in a house but in the tombs. ²⁸When he saw Jesus, he cried out, fell down before Him, and with a loud voice said, "What have I to do with You, Jesus, Son of the Most High God? I beg You, do not torment me!" ²⁹For He had commanded the unclean spirit to come out of the man. For it had often seized him, and he was kept under guard, bound with chains and shackles; and he broke the bonds and was driven by the demon into the wilderness.

³⁰Jesus asked him, saying, "What is your name?"

And he said, "Legion," because many demons had entered him. ³¹And they begged Him that He would not command them to go out into the abyss.

³²Now a herd of many swine was feeding there on the mountain. So they begged Him that He would permit them to enter them. And He permitted them. ³³Then the demons went out of the man and entered the swine, and the herd ran violently down the steep place into the lake and drowned.

³⁴When those who fed *them* saw what had happened, they fled and told *it* in the city and in the country. ³⁵Then they went out to see what had happened, and came to Jesus, and found the man from whom the demons had departed, sitting at the feet of Jesus, clothed and in his right mind. And they were afraid. ³⁶They also who had seen *it* told them by what means he who had been demon-possessed was healed. ³⁷Then the whole multitude of the surrounding region of the Gadarenes[d] asked Him to depart from them, for they were seized with great fear. And He got into the boat and returned.

³⁸Now the man from whom the demons had departed begged Him that he might be with Him. But Jesus sent him away, saying, ³⁹"Return to your own house, and tell what great things God has done for you." And he went his way and proclaimed throughout the whole city what great things Jesus had done for him.

(NKJV)

7) John 11: 38-44

Lazarus Raised from the Dead

³⁸Then Jesus, again groaning in Himself, came to the tomb. It was a cave, and a stone lay against it. ³⁹Jesus said, "Take away the stone."

Martha, the sister of him who was dead, said to Him, "Lord, by this time there is a stench, for he has been *dead* four days."

⁴⁰Jesus said to her, "Did I not say to you that if you would believe you would see the glory of God?"

[41] Then they took away the stone *from the place* where the dead man was lying.[a] And Jesus lifted up *His* eyes and said, "Father, I thank You that You have heard Me. [42] And I know that You always hear Me, but because of the people who are standing by I said *this,* that they might believe that You sent Me." [43] Now when He had said these things, He cried with a loud voice, "Lazarus, come forth!" [44] And he who had died came out bound hand and foot with graveclothes, and his face was wrapped with a cloth. Jesus said to them, "Loose him, and let him go."

(NKJV)